I0477707

TECHNICAL ANALYSIS OF STOCK TRENDS

INVESMENT SERIES
CONCISE READS™

PETER OLIVER

TECHNICAL ANALYSIS OF STOCK TRENDS
Copyright © 2019 by Concise Reads™

CONTENTS

INTRODUCTION   5

TECHNICAL ANALYSIS   9

PROFESSIONAL DESIGNATIONS   11

BRIEF HISTORY OF TECHNICAL ANALYSIS   12

CHARLES H. DOW   13

THE DOW THEORY   16

SECTION 1   28

TYPES OF CHARTS   29

TRENDLINES   34

SUPPORT & RESISTANCE   37

MOVING AVERAGES   41

VOLUME WEIGHTED AVERAGE PRICE   43

MOVING AVERAGE CROSSOVER   46

MACD   48

RSI   51

CHART READING   56

SECTION TWO   61

CANDLESTICK READINGS   61

THE DOJIS   65

CHART PATTERN RECOGNITION   67

CONTINUATION PATTERNS   68

REVERSAL PATTERNS   72

PRICE TARGETS   76

GAPS   79

FIBONACCI SEQUENCE   84

RE-ENTRY & THE TURTLE TRADERS   89

RISK MANAGEMENT   92

CONCLUSION   94

ADDITIONAL MATERIAL   97

INTRODUCTION

I started trading in 2003 before opening an account in 2006 with Zecco, one of the early discount brokerage firms which later merged with TradeKing, which itself was acquired by Ally Invest in 2016. Prior to taking the plunge into trading, I read everything I could about strategies and "best" practices. Knowing that there would be a learning curve, I initially limited myself to $2000. I started with options and equities, then moved to the pink sheets, or significantly discounted (under a dollar and usually under one cent) stocks that did not meet the minimum requirements to be listed on a major exchange. The pink sheets used to be the publication of the prices for the over the counter (OTC) stocks. Today we call them penny stocks. I used recent company news and technical analysis to turn $2000 into $48,000 in 18 months. I then lost half that value during the beginning of the financial crisis forcing me to pull my money out until I could come up with a better plan on how to tackle the bear market. The bear market beat me, but I knew that there was money to be made. I just needed a different strategy. I realized then that penny stocks were so thinly traded (low volume) that my analyses worked sometimes, but not most of the time. I didn't have enough data with penny stocks to build a strategy that worked. Additionally, it was taking time away from my graduate studies at the time and I needed to re-evaluate what my relationship with the stock market was going to be in the long run. After careful consideration, I had decided that my time horizon was days and weeks not minutes and hours and so I re-adjusted the timeframe windows for my trading strategy so that I was focusing on mid-term to longer term trends. I then followed the financials over the next several weeks. I forecasted where the bottom would be for a variety of financial stocks, and in 2008 and 2009 had 300-400% returns in a matter of weeks for each stock I invested in. The strategy I was using to make money is often referred to as "bottom-feeding" or "value investing". I used fundamental analysis to determine the intrinsic value for a stock and used that as a gauge when buying and selling during the financial crisis. While my value investing worked during the tail end of the bear market--the bull market came and my strategy stopped working. Every stock was hitting new 52 week highs. There were no longer term bottoms or 'value' stocks to invest in. I shifted my strategy to focus much more on momentum indicators but this time I did something differently. Instead of concerning myself with individual company stocks, I focused on larger more liquid ETFs. I decided that I wasn't going to waste anymore more time screening for stocks, and I picked 20 ETFs that

I started to follow over the next 10 years. I reserved about 10% of my portfolio for my gambling habit which included more recently investing in Cannabis stocks (Aurora, Aphria, and the MJ or MaryJane ETF). I would switch ETFs over the years whenever I noticed that my strategy was not working as well relative to the others in my ETF universe. I don't short the market, and that is why I hold a few inverse ETFs for some of my best performing ETFs. I've found success, but as I am finding less and less time to study charts, I am building an automated trader that uses my personal strategies to trade for me as if it were me. These are available with Fidelity, Interactive Brokers, and a number of brokerage firms but you have to meet certain minimum requirements to do so. Even with the automated trader using my technical analysis strategies, I still have to check on its performance from time to time.

What the past 15 years have taught me is that if we try hard enough we will find patterns in anything we look at it whether we're talking about stocks or a phenomenon in nature. Having said that, patterns come and go. Patterns don't exist forever. This is a very important lesson. Throughout this guide, you'll learn new concepts and new techniques for technical trading. However, it is highly likely that you'll only end up using one or two indicators to help you decide whether to buy or sell. There are many veteran traders who ONLY use the RSI indicator for example. Others only use the 50-day and

200-day moving average. That's the extent of their technical trading. You will find something that works consistently for the types of charts you are looking at. There are too many variables to know exactly what charts your eye is attracted to, but it could be 1 week timeframe healthcare stocks in emerging markets between the years of 2019 and 2021. That's just a very specific example. The point is that you will find something that works, and if it's accurate more than 50% of the time, then you have the opportunity to actually make a living trading your strategy as so many traders have done in the past, either part-time or full-time.

TECHNICAL ANALYSIS

Technical analysis is what I want you to use for the bulk of your active trading, and fundamental analysis should be reserved for a small portion of your portfolio for stocks in an industry you really *really* know well. While fundamental analysis looks at a company's fundamentals or their publicly available financial statements, technical analysis on the other hand is an analysis of the price movement of the stock regardless of what the fundamentals are saying. Technical analysis doesn't care about the fundamentals of a company. Even if the company has stellar profit margins, lower debt, and higher growth than its competitors, if the majority are selling the stock then it's price will go down. With technical analysis we are looking at the price movement as a reflection of the underlying belief of the majority of purchasing power trading a particular stock, and hence it is used in what is known as 'momentum' trading which follows the momentum of the stock. You might have heard of the old adage of buy low and sell high. Well, please only believe that when you are using fundamental analysis on the few stocks you really see a long term growth potential. For everything else, buy high and sell higher. The unfortunate premise behind success with momentum trading is to make sure you are not the last one holding the bag or in other words you are not the last person to sell a momentum stock because by that point everyone else has sold and the price already declined significantly, likely below your buying price. We'll learn in this guide that this happens a lot, and you'll need to decide on your exit or sell strategy before you buy a particular stock in order to limit your losses in case things don't go as you predicted. The goal with technical analysis is to be right more times than you are wrong. Even being 55% right and 45% wrong with equal investments each time means you'll make a profit at the end of the year.

PROFESSIONAL DESIGNATIONS

Professionals who focus on fundamental analysis end up studying for a 1000 hour exam known as the CFA or certified financial analyst exam. Other professionals who focus on technical analysis, especially day traders who trade the same stock multiple times a day could study for the CMT designation or the Charter Market Technician. There are only 2400 CMTs employed by the major financial advisory banks (Morgan Stanley, Fidelity, Charles Schwab, among others). Hedge Funds hire physics and statistics PhDs to codify trading strategies using a mix of technical and fundamental analysis. These quantitative strategies are considered the firm's intellectual property, and millions are invested in cyber and physical security limiting access in and out of the server rooms. Neither the CFA or the CMT are required to start trading your own money.

BRIEF HISTORY OF TECHNICAL ANALYSIS

CHARLES H. DOW

Charles Dow started out as a journalist, but he will forever be remembered as one of the pioneers of technical analysis. Dow was born in Sterling, Connecticut on November 6, 1851. He was the son of a farmer who found work as a journalist at the age of 21 in nearby Massachusetts with the Springfield Daily Republican. He worked there for three years before moving to Rhode Island to join the Providence Star which he soon left after two more years to join the Providence Journal. It was there that he met his boss George W. Danielson, the editor, who was so impressed with Dow's thorough research and reporting that he asked him to join a group of Wall Street financiers on their trip to Colorado to evaluate investments in silver mining. He was an observant and talkative young man who gained the confidence of the investors on the trip and invited them to share with him what <u>information</u> was useful and what was not for wall street investors. It was a short four day trip, but Dow learned a key lesson and that is that information, the right information, is what turns a risky investment into a multimillion dollar profit. Soon after that trip, in 1880 at the age of 29 years old Dow moved to New York and joined the Kiernan Wall Street Financial News Bureau as a reporter. He now had the chance to search for valuable information and see what effect it had on the stock price. Two short years later, now at the age of 31 years old, Dow partnered with his long time friend and Brown university dropout, Edward Davis Jones, to establish the Dow, Jones & Company financial news bureau which published a two page financial news daily summary for the next 7 years. In 1889, the young company decided to publish a full fledged newspaper and called it the Wall Street Journal. Yes, THE Wall Street Journal we read today. 7 years after that in 1896, the Dow Jones Industrial Average (DJIA) was created which was made up of the sum of the closing prices of 12 companies divided by 12 to get an average.

He taught us that markets trend (up or down) and that this trend can be predicted by looking at indices or the average price of a collection of companies that fairly represent the economy. Dow believed that industrials (the DJIA) and railroad transportation (the index was created a year later in 1897) were the core engines of the economy, if these failed, then the economy failed and vice versa. Of course this is not necessarily true today especially for railroad transportation being considered the core engine of the economy, but the signalling theory persists. This means that if the Dow Jones Industrial Average (DJIA) which he created is dropping, then news anchors everywhere start spreading 'news' that the 'market is down', this in turn likely affects the behavior of risk averse investors and actually causes the market beyond industrials to dip lower.

THE DOW
THEORY

Dow theory is a theory of price movement based on 255 editorials that Charles Dow wrote in his publication, the Wall Street Journal. After his death in 1902, it went through several updates to remain relevant. The ideas in the Dow theory have been echoed multiple times throughout the past century, albeit in slightly different time frames and with emphasis the ideas that are more noteworthy. The important takeaway is to understand what Dow understood which is that there seems to be a repeating pattern when it comes to humans investing in stocks. Human behavior hasn't changed for, well forever, and so these patterns are expected to continue to repeat forever. Understand that fundamental assumption, and you'll be able to pick and choose which parts you believe in the Dow Theory. My opinion is that Dow was correct in assuming a pattern exists. His timing of these patterns may or may not be a little off and other traders such as Gann observed more nuanced patterns. I don't want you to memorize how long a bull period is because that will just force you to take it as truth and not realize that human behavior although repetitive can be different in different economic, political, and even environmental conditions. You will start noticing patterns as you gain experience but only if you are looking for new patterns.

The six tenants of the Dow Theory are as follows:

1. **Markets follow multiple cycles at the same time**. First, markets have a **long term** primary movement or major trend whether bullish or bearish. This is followed by a **medium term** secondary reaction that retraces ⅓ to ⅔ OR 33% to 67% of the previous price. This can be in either direction--bullish or bearish. This is then followed by a **short swing** or minor movement which also retraces the stock price but to a smaller degree. You can imagine that a market could have a long term bullish trend such as from March 2009 to 2017 with a medium swing in 2015 and 2016 and multiple short swings along the way. This is a very insightful observation. You can see multiple trends by zooming in and out on the Dow Jones price chart.

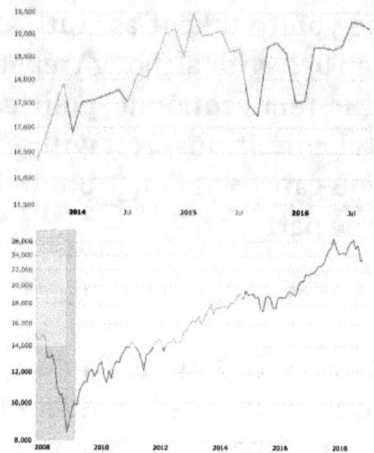

DJIA short term trend and long term smoothing

An extension of the first tenant of the Dow theory is that not only do we see different long term and short term patterns depending on how long or how short of a time period we focus on, BUT there are also different patterns when we change the interval of our data points. We can look at any time period using any interval from 1 minute to 1 year. The longer 4 hour interval for example smooths out the multiple short term trends seen in the 1 hour interval chart. We'll discuss this more, and the important takeaway is that yes patterns do exist. Our indicators for these patterns are not always correct because despite humans behaving the same to the same stimuli, the environmental stimuli are similar but never exactly the same as prior periods. If that wasn't clear, re-read it again until it does make sense. Lastly, when we change the time interval from a longer time interval to a shorter one, we can either see a pattern we didn't see before OR end up increasing the statistical noise which is another way of saying that we end up obscuring a pattern we identified in the longer time interval.

The choice of time intervals comes with experience but I'll simplify one approach. Assume that it takes 10 to 20 periods or data points for some form of pattern to emerge to let you know if you should buy or sell. If we choose a 1 min interval as day traders do, then we may get a signal every 10 to 20 minutes. On the other, I have several businesses I need to pay attention to and so can only trade once a day or every few days. To accommodate my lifestyle, I use the 4-hour, 12-hour, and 24-hour time intervals. This gives me a few days to a few weeks between trades, and that suits my lifestyle. There's no way of knowing for sure whether I would be more profitable trading more or less frequently, and so I don't bother thinking about it given that I am grateful for what works for me.

This reminds me of a story I read a few years ago, I believe it was in 2009. This was the story of an average 9 to 5 office employee who had terrible luck in the stock market. He then learned technical analysis but could never find a good set up in the stocks he was following and did not have the time to screen thousands of stocks because he worked full time. That was until one day he overheard some of his co-workers talking excitedly to each other about this amazing book they were reading. He didn't read books nor did he intend to, but still, he went home and asked his friends and his wife if they ever heard of the book the Hunger Games. Everyone he talked to seemed excited about it. He googled if the movie rights to the book were sold in the past year. They were, and he invested in that company's stock. He waited almost a year without much price movement until finally the news broke out that the movie was a blockbuster hit. He made a small fortune on a hunch. Keep in mind he could have lost a lot of money if the movie flopped and he did wait a year until there was any price action in the stock. Still it worked for him so he did it again after he overheard his teenagers get excited about this new app everyone was using. Three years later he can officially call himself a millionaire. To protect his privacy, I'm not sharing additional details. The reason I like this story is because he was betting, took a few gambles, and they paid off.

Gambling can be a lot of fun for the non-addict BUT only with a tiny portion of your assets.

It's great to have a hunch and to watch your hunch pay off. There's a sense of deserved accomplishment. Asymmetry of information builds confidence and the payoff could be substantial but never put your eggs in the same basket. The gentleman I'm describing is lucky because he invested in a bull market--everything was going up on the slightest positive news. If he had decided to put money in 2007 or late 2018, he would have lost it regardless of the performance of the movie. I hope for his sake he looked at the long term trend or the short term momentum trend and decided to stay out regardless of how optimistic the wealth advisors and news anchors were.

Before we move on to the next tenant of Dow Theory, just remember that your first goal is to <u>decide</u> if the market is in an **uptrend** with higher highs, a **downtrend** with lower lows, or in a **sideways trend**. Get that right, then everything else stems from this first step.

2. **Market primary (long-term) trends exist in 3 phases:** The three phases follow a pattern of behavior. The investors that have the right information early are usually a minority, and they buy up as much as the market is willing to sell. This doesn't move the price up because they are a minority number of investors who are buying (or selling short) and adding to their total number of shares. This period where the stock neither goes up or down is known as **accumulation**. Next, other people start catching on, and some news articles are coming out with the positive or negative news. At that point, the **absorption** or **public participation** phase occurs and the stock price moves quickly up or down. Finally, once the public has bought in (or

sold), the early investors sell (or buy) shares while the rest of the public start seeing the trend reversing and their profits quickly turning negative. This is known as the **distribution** phase.

Economists believe that markets are efficient which is also known as the **efficient market hypothesis** or that all information is available to all investors at the same time and it is *impossible* to beat the market. Despite that theory, we tend to see a pattern of accumulation even today before a major news release and it can't be all explained by insider trading. Ergo--the market must be inefficient because someone knows something that someone else does not yet know. Think of the cryptocurrency or the cannabis mania, there were a lot of millionaires created and a lot of people who were left with a loss holding on to stock in the distribution phase. I am not saying we know how or why this happens, only that there is a pattern and that pattern happens frequently. This is what Dow observed more than a century ago.

The bull market cycles are accumulation> public participation (until the peak)> distribution. In a bull market it is known as a 'rally' while in a bear market it is known as a 'sell-off'. If we all had the same information at the same time, then the timing between these phases would be so small, few if any would be able to profit. In momentum trading we try to detect accumulation and predict the public participation phase.

3. **The Stock Market Averages Must Confirm Each Other:** As mentioned earlier, Dow believed the core engines of the economy were industrials and transportation. If indices for both are going up in price then the economy as a whole is bullish but if they are diverging from each other then the economy could be in the beginning of a contraction. This tenant is semi plausible if taken at face value but if we understand the insight driving this conclusion then we can utilize it to get a global feel for the markets. Dow was focusing on the drivers of the economy during his time.

Extrapolated to serve our purposes, if we are looking at APPLE's stock, and we find in their annual 10-K report that a big portion of their revenue comes from China. That is a core engine in their stock price. Well, if competition in China ever increased or trade relations weakened and China imposed increased taxes or tariffs on Apple products (which would consequently increase competition) then their annual revenue forecasts would inevitably decrease leading to a decrease in their stock price. Similarly, if you are investing in mortgage companies such as Fannie or Freddie then you would quickly find out that its core engine is the interest rate level. Higher than expected interest rate increases means fewer home buyers which means fewer insured mortgages which cause a decrease in the stock price. While this might seem like fundamental analysis, it can actually be both fundamental or technical. A technical trader would notice momentum changes or divergence in a complimentary market and use that to predict a change in trend in the stock they are following.

Annual (10-K) and Quarterly (8-K) reports are available on all public companies using the EDGAR search engine on the SEC website. Just type 'SEC EDGAR' into google and it'll show up as one of the first page links.

4. **The Stock Market Discounts All News:** This is Dow essentially agreeing that news factor into the price almost instantaneously, so that it is impossible to beat the market waiting for the news except if you are selling the news. One thing to keep in mind as you digest this tenant is that Dow's short term trend was several weeks long and the long term trend he looked at could be up to a decade long. Having such long time horizons would make it seem natural that news are automatically and instantaneously priced into the stock price. However, that's not true for shorter term horizons in my experience. This is a good example of how your perspective shapes your reality. In this case, perspective is the time horizon chosen. The two examples we mentioned previously regarding Apple getting news of increased competition in China, or Fannie and Freddie facing an interest rate increase by the Federal Reserve, are what we call unexpected news.

Expected news is priced in months in advance. Unexpected news causes a rapid market reaction that would never be caught using a longer time horizon such as those that Dow focused on. If Apple had to cut its revenue forecast because of increased competition in China and a diminishing market share, then that news would take several hours and potentially days before the stock price finally bottomed out. The first group of investors to sell or short the stock would come out as the winners. Better yet, the ones who followed the revenue forecasts of Apple's competitors would have sold before the news even came out. In fact, Apple's stock would be in a downward momentum, albeit small in magnitude, days and weeks before the news came out. In essence, does the stock market discount all news? Yes in the sense that the majority of price change occurs SOON AFTER the news is released, but no in the sense that there is still an opportunity for profit for a minority of investors. If you are an average investor, it may be hard to keep track of changes in the core engines of a stock's price, and if you are not a day trader, it may be even harder to make a profit during the rapid momentum change right after the news comes out. As a swing trader, I always use stop losses based on twice the volatility of a stock. Stop losses sell at a specific price just in the event of these unexpected news that could hurt my investment. The volatility indicator I use is the **Average True Range**, and we will cover that in this guide, and you should consider using it to protect your investment and minimize any losses.

This is an important reminder to emphasize that for whatever reason, retirement accounts don't utilize stop losses very well. When the economy crashes, people's retirement accounts lose all the gains they made in the prior decade. I invest directly from my retirement account and in 2018 I was out of the market by September and prevented significant potential losses that would have occurred in October, November, and December.

> Stop Losses—the most widely used
> tool of technical traders.

5. **Volume Confirms Trends:** Price is half the story. Price can go up and down with very little volume which means a minority of investors are bullish or bearish but that trend won't be sustained unless the majority of investors are on board. Volume is relative--remember that. When looking at volume you are not looking at the absolute volume but at the volume relative to average volume.

6. **Trends Persist Until They Don't:** This sounds like a Yogi Berra saying. If you are not familiar with Yogi Berra he was a baseball player who was quoted saying the most obvious statements for which a minority of people believe that although obvious, his sayings had deep meaningful insights.

A famous Yogi-ism is "It ain't over till it's over."

Dow is actually being insightful here. He is echoing Newton's First Law of Motion which states that a body at rest will remain at rest and a body in motion will stay in motion unless acted on by outside force. In technical analysis, a trend persists until a new trend occurs, and importantly when one trend stops another must appear. We have either an uptrend, a downtrend, or a horizontal trend. Even a horizontal trend will at any one point have an uptrend or a downtrend if we zoom in to a smaller time interval. The grey area that technical investors can disagree on is when to call a new trend. Technical analysts often use multiple indicators so that if two indicators signal a trend reversal then they are confident, and if three indicators agree there is a trend reversal then they are even more confident. Of course, there is an old saying that if too many indicators agree then you're already too late to profit and the price change has already occurred. One important observation to note is that while there are multiple momentum indicators than can indicate trend reversal, when compared to the longer term trend, it can be sometimes difficult to tell if the trend reversal is simply a correction with continuation of the primary trend or a true reversal of the primary trend. This distinction has not been clearly identified but with practice and a passion for learning, you will find that you can be right more often than you are wrong in spotting that distinction.

SECTION 1

TYPES OF CHARTS

There are four common types of charts. Line, bar, candlestick, and point & figure charts.

Line charts are exactly what they sound like. The only caveat is that the price data points used are ONLY the closing prices for each period. Line charts are used because they are easy to understand, but they don't contain a lot of information especially since price can have <u>4 different data points</u> in each period.

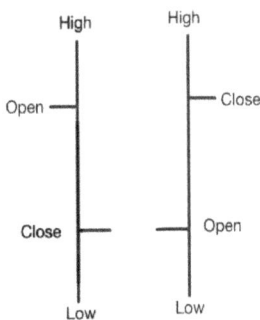

The **Bar chart** shows a bar for any given period. Remember the period can be anything from 1 minute to 1 week. You decide what period you want to look at. Each bar shows 4 price data points which are the highest price in a period, the lowest price, the open price and the close price. These 'Western' bar charts are also known as OHLC charts because they depict the open, high, low, and close prices. A branch to the left denotes an open price and a branch to the right denotes a close price.

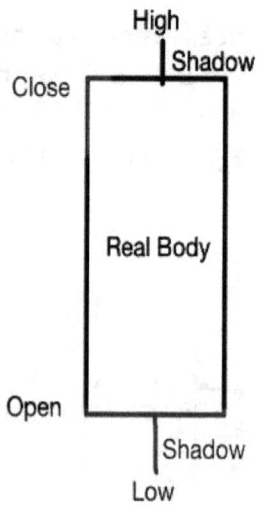

The **Japanese candlesticks** are similar to the bar but are more visual (read: prettier). Filled and empty bars make it visually appealing to spot whether the closing price is above or below the opening price. A filled bar means the close price is <u>lower</u> than the open price while an empty bar means the close price is <u>higher</u> than the open price. The color Green compares the closing price for a given candlestick to the closing price of the previous candlestick. A GREEN HOLLOW candlestick is bullish because the closing price is higher than the previous period AND the closing price is higher than the opening price. A RED FILLED candlestick is bearish because the closing price is lower than the previous period closing price AND the closing price is below the opening price. The other two options for these visual candlesticks are a GREEN FILLED candlestick which shows a slowing uptrend and potential for bearish reversal and a RED HOLLOW candlestick which shows a slowing downtrend and potential for a bullish reversal.

Price				
10	X		X	O
9	X	O	X	O
8	X	O		O
7	X			
6	X			
5	X			

Point and Figure charts or P&F charts were reportedly originally used by Charles Dow and others at the turn of the century. They were useful in that they allowed chartists to record price movement very quickly and still presented momentum information. In Fact, in the early 20th century, P&F chartists could complete 50 to 100 charts in a single working day all by hand. Some traders still use these today. More recently (in history), Tom Dorsey, founder of the research firm Dorsey, Wright & Associates (1987) authored several books on spotting trends using P&F charts. We won't spend a lot of time in this concise guide on P&F charts, suffice it to say that it interestingly modifies the price chart to clarify <u>volatility</u>. The P&F charts usually have price on the y axis but do not have time in the x-axis as traditional charts do. Additionally, instead of charting prices, it sets a box size defined by the trader and records an 'X' if the price moved up by that range or an 'O' if it moved down by that range. In the example above, if the price moved up by three boxes, then three X's are recorded in three boxes moving up the price axis. If the next day the price moves up again by another three boxes, then another three X's are recorded. If on the third day, the price reversed by two boxes, then a new column with two 'O's is recorded. The fourth and final day in this example, the price goes up again but this time by two boxes followed by dropping back down by three boxes. Just by looking at this simple example, we can see there is uptrend with support at a price of $8 and resistance at a price of $10. With enough data, we can also tell whether volatility is three boxes or two boxes which helps us set our price targets for uncharted territory without support or resistance levels. I don't use P&F charts, but I took the insight that the delta or change in price is much more interesting than the absolute value of price when looking at a chart and have used it for example to draw the percentage returns of different indices such as the S&P 500 which I show in the first guide in the series, the "Investing for Retirement' guide.

TRENDLINES

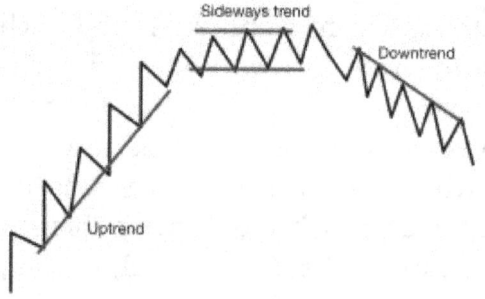

Trend lines are lines connecting price points along a price chart. Sounds simple enough. To draw an uptrend we would connect the lowest points or **troughs** of each price movement. This trend line shows the support level that would maintain this upward trend. The trend continues when the price comes close to the trend line but bounces back up. When the price breaks the trend line, it is said to <u>break the trend</u>.

Similarly, to draw a downtrend we would connect the highest points or **peaks** of each price move-ment. This trendline would then represent the resistance levels where if the trend continues as expected then the price points would come close to the trendline but soon rebound lower. When the price breaks above the trendline, that is a bullish sign for a new uptrend.

There are too many false positive breakouts to use trendlines alone as an indicator of a potential trend reversal. Some traders take advantage of that fact and actually buy the dips when price breaks <u>below</u> an uptrend assuming that it will soon break back <u>above</u> the uptrend line. In other words, they are betting against the false positives.

The fun part of drawing trendlines is that you can more clearly illustrate the trend within a few seconds. In fact, you could find a trend within a trend such that the long term trend connecting the large troughs together is an uptrend but there are a few periods where each peak was lower than the previous one indicating a shorter term downtrend.

There is no point to belabor how to draw lines. From experience, I have noticed that when a price movement significantly breaks a trend, many traders continue to use the original trendline to predict a reverse breakout back through the trendline. Personally, I believe that how long ago a break occurred is good enough to tell us whether that original trend is no longer the primary trend. For example, if I drew a trendline that ranged for 20 periods and the break through the trendline has lasted more than 5 periods, let's say 10 periods, then I would draw a **new** trendline to get more accurate support and resistance levels. Often times, I find that the new trend is flat or a horizontal trend and I turn out to be right. When the new trend is horizontal, I sell my position and don't return until there is either an uptrend or a downtrend (if I choose to short the stock or buy put options). Some sectors can stay in a horizontal trend for years, and it is a good idea to rotate to another sector that has an uptrend or downtrend.

SUPPORT & RESISTANCE

We briefly talked about how trend lines can be used as support during an uptrend and resistance during a downtrend. We can also find specific price points that act as support and resistance. Psychologically, traders love round numbers, and we often find support or resistance in nice round numbers such as $10 instead of $10.45 as support and $12 as resistance instead of $12.03. The support is the price point where buyers overwhelm sellers. If a stock price chart drops to $10 for example and bounces back, then there were more buyers than sellers at that price point (technically more buying POWER than selling POWER). If the price action repeats itself AGAIN, then we have a stronger support level. The more times it tests that support level and bounces back the more buyers we have in the market at that price level. The same holds true when deciding which price point to call a resistance level. If a stock price comes close to $12 for example and retreats then repeats this price action again a second time, then we have a resistance level at $12. If the price action breaks through the support to reach a lower price level, then we have a bearish signal that the stock price will continue to decrease. Similarly, if the stock price breaks a resistance level, then it is a bullish signal.

Keep in mind that if the price action tests a support level too many times and more often than it tests the resistance level above, then it is only a matter of time before it breaks the support level. The same holds true with the resistance level. This means, if you see a price action testing the resistance level multiple times but not testing the support level, this should give you insight on market behavior. Specifically, buyers are keeping up the momentum but there are not enough buyers to overwhelm the sellers. Soon the sellers will have sold all their stock, and the buyers will overwhelm the sellers and break the resistance level. When a resistance is broken, it then becomes a new support level because that is where buyers bought in. This is confirmed the next time the price action touches the new support line and bounces back. This is known as the **polarity principle**. The same takes place where a support level becomes a resistance level once support is broken and confirmed in subsequent price action.

The polarity principle belief is based on the assumption that when a new resistance level is broken for example, there must have been more buyers than sellers at that price point on the chart and so these new crop of buyers would not sell near the same price they bought in and this becomes a new support level. Does it always hold true? No. If there is a market crash or panic, then investors would rather sell at a small loss rather than a large loss and the support is maybe held for a few minutes. More conservative traders would only call a price level a support if the price point reached that support level and bounced back. More conservative traders would only call that same price point a support if the price bounced back up at least twice. The more buyers at the support level, the stronger the support level is because of the assumption that the average investors will likely not sell at the same price they originally bought the stock.

When looking at support and resistance, we find that we are reading market behavior. We'll learn more about reading market behavior when we look at a few candlestick patterns and later when we learn about the common chart patterns. For now, just keep the perspective that you are not attempting to beat the market with momentum trading, but rather you are attempting to understand what is happening between the bulls (buyers) and the bears (sellers) and put your money on the most likely winner. Your number one insight into market behavior is price. All the technical analyses subsequent to that is to confirm your insight from the price action.

Okay, so we learned that the first insight we need to have is know the **primary trend** of the stock chart and that can be done visually or in a matter of seconds using trendlines. We then decide on the **support** and **resistance** levels which as we learned can be at a specific price points but we can use the trendlines as support and resistance levels. More traditional traders have used moving averages to tell them what the trend and the support/resistance levels, while more sophisticated traders have used a moving average known as the VWAP to identify the trend as well as the support/resistance levels. Let's look at those next.

MOVING AVERAGES

AAPL 2015-2018

Moving averages are a smoothing function to get rid of the random fluctuations in price in order to clarify the overall trend. Moving averages are trend-lines that are calculated by getting the average of a number of prior periods. A period of 10 using a 1 day time interval refers to the last 10 days. If you switch the window to a 1 hour time interval, a period of 10 will now reflect the average of the last 10 hours. It is moving because the average is dynamic since the number of periods it uses is fixed. For example, let's say we use a window of 1-day, which means each period is 1 day long. If we choose the 50 day moving average, then we are dividing the sum of the price for the last 50 periods by 50. This is known as a Simple Moving Average or SMA. If we move forward one day, the moving average updates by dropping the last price and adding the new price to have a trailing 50 periods. A simple moving average gives equal weight to every period used in calculating, while an exponential moving average gives more weight to the more recent period. In the figure above we see the price chart for Apple (AAPL) between 2015 and 2018. We see that the **exponential moving average** or **EMA** more closely hugs the price line compared to the SMA because it reacts faster due to weighing more recent prices higher. This same principle applies so that the shorter the moving average period, the more it hugs the price line until you have a period of one at which point the moving average of period one is the price itself.

Importantly, the price data point chosen is usually the closing price for a period but <u>price</u> in any single period can be the **opening price**, the **low price**, the **high price**, or the **closing price**. Personally, I prefer to use the <u>high price</u> for a *buy* signal moving average and the <u>low price</u> for a *sell* signal moving average. The moving averages can be used by themselves to reflect trend or to signal buy and sell opportunities by seeing if the moving average breaks a price resistance or a price support level. Similar buy and sell opportunities using moving averages are found in the **MACD** or Moving Average Convergence Divergence indicator.

VOLUME WEIGHTED AVERAGE PRICE

AAPL 2013-2018

The **VWAP** unlike the simple or exponential moving averages uses volume to weigh the price action. For example, let's say 500 shares of AAPL were bought at $165 in one period, then 700 shares of AAPL were bought at $166 in the next period, and 300 shares of AAPL were bought at $167. The three period VWAP in this case would be:

$$(500*165)+(700*166)+(300*167) / 1500\text{-shares}$$

This gives us a VWAP of $165.87 as compared to a simple moving average of $166. The VWAP looks at **money flow**. It looks at money coming in and going out and so it is a more reliable trendline to use for support and resistance than moving averages are because it's weighed using the actual number of shares bought/sold for a given price point.

The Anchored VWAP allows us to anchor to a specific date and time in the price chart. What is shown in the price chart of AAPL above between 2013 and 2018 are two anchored VWAPs-- one anchored to June, 2013 or the beginning of an uptrend, and the second shorter curve is anchored to June 2016 also the beginning of an uptrend. The point I'm trying to make here is that anchored VWAPs are only helpful if you anchor them to the most recent trend you are following. Once a new trend takes place, the anchored VWAP is too far off to matter and the buyers and sellers from the first trend may not be the same buyers and sellers in the more recent trend you are reviewing. In the example of AAPL, if we had used the anchored VWAP from 2013, we wouldn't sell but if we used a more recent anchored VWAP that represent the buyers of the most recent uptrend, we would see that once the price action crossed the VWAP or our support, then it was time to sell. We see the bears took over and now would be a good time to draw a new trendline for the downtrend.

Therefore, for trendlines, moving averages, or VWAPs that are used as support or resistance, the general assumption is that if price is > price average then that is bullish and if price < price average then that is a bearish signal. When an uptrending price crosses below the price average then that is a bearish reversal, and if a downtrending price crosses above the price average then that is a bullish reversal.

MOVING AVERAGE CROSSOVER

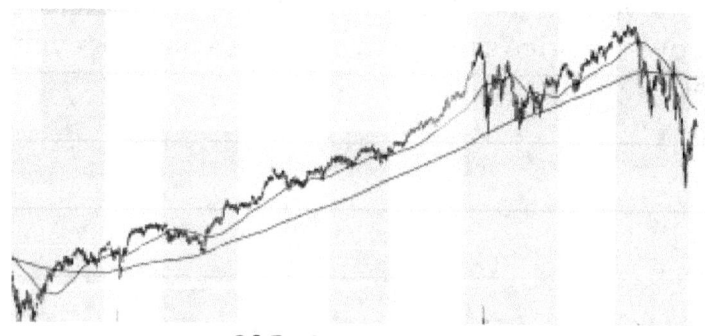

S&P500 2016-2018

Let's get back to the discussion of trends. Moving averages are very commonly compared to predict short term trend reversals. Some of the oldest technical traders are happy and achieve their desired returns by using only the 50 day and the 200 day moving average. If the shorter 50 day moving average crosses above the 200 day moving average then that is a bullish signal that after another several periods the 200 day moving average will follow the uptrend. If the shorter 50 day moving average crosses below the 200 day moving average, then that is a bearish signal that after several more periods the 200 day moving average will show the same downtrend. Why not just follow the 50 day moving average since it is shorter and more re-active? Well, if you want to get a feel for the longer term trends in the market, then it helps to see if the price action is overall bullish or overall bear-ish, and it is the relative action of the shorter and longer term moving averages that can give us this forecast. In the S&P 500 price chart above we see the 50 day moving average cross over the 200 day moving average in March, 2016 and stay above it until December, 2018. As long as the 50 day moving average remained above the 200 day moving aver-age, we can see the S&P 500 price continue in an uptrend between March 2016 and September 2018. October 2018 is when the 50 day moving average curve began downtrending and also when the S&P 500 began its steep decline.

MACD

Moving Average Convergence Divergence is a directional momentum indicator that takes what we've been doing manually with moving average crossover for short term and long term moving averages to decide when to buy or sell and automates it for us with a nice curve. The MACD calculation uses 3 moving averages with 3 different periods that need to be set. The traditional periods used are 12, 26, and 9 days. The first is a fast 12-period EMA, the second is a slow 26-period EMA, and the third is a 9-period EMA called the 'signal line'. The MACD line is the EMA 12 minus EMA 26 which tells us if the fast trend is moving up or down relative to the slow trend and by how much. As with moving average crossovers, we expect that an uptrend will show a positive MACD and a downtrend will show a negative MACD. The MACD line is then plotted against the shorter signal line. The buy signal is when MACD crosses above the signal line and the sell signal is when the MACD crosses below the signal line. The distance between the MACD line and the signal line is shown as a histogram. If the distance is positive or the MACD>signal line then the histogram shows positive values, and if the MACD<signal line then the histogram shows negative values. The MACD in my opinion has been fundamental to my trading. I changed the histogram slightly to clarify when the distance between the MACD and the signal line is moving from negative or less positive to more positive. This is important and we'll see how I use it next.

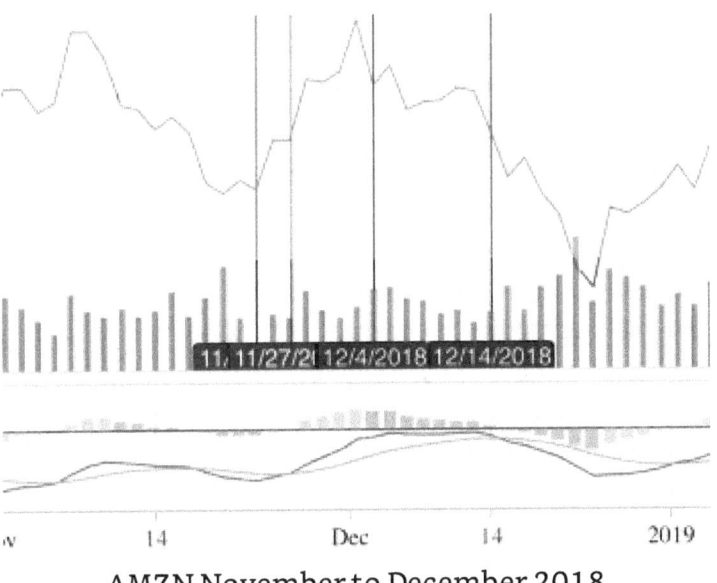

AMZN November to December 2018

Using MACD(12,26,9) we see that when MACD crosses above the signal line (11/27/2018), the price action is in an uptrend and similarly when the MACD crosses below the signal line (12/14/2018) the price action is in a downtrend. These are good buy and sell signals respectively but as we can tell from the graph, they catch the uptrend and down-trend a little after the fact. Instead, if we use the sign change of the MACD line from negative to posi-tive or for the math geeks when the first deriva-tive is zero AND the second derivative (the slope of the slope) is > 0 (meaning the next slope will be positive) then we can catch the uptrend in the beginning. The same applies to the sell signal. I drew some lines to show my method. The first ver-tical line shows when we would buy if we used this method and the third line (12/04/2018) shows when we would have sold using this strategy. Now, for the non math geeks, the easier alternative is to look at the histogram. When the histogram changes from red to green, that is when the slope of the MACD just turned positive and the slope is greater than the signal line which means the next bar in the histogram will be larger as the distance between the MACD and the signal line continues to increase. Now when the histogram turns red or reaches a peak and then starts decreasing in size we know that the slope of the MACD is less positive than the signal line and that is a good sell signal. This has worked for me, it may not work for you. If this is confusing, take your time and reread this section.

RSI

The Relative Strength Indicator measures the relative strength of price action. It is a momentum indicator because it tells us whether the bulls or bears are winning. It is a momentum **oscillator** because its value oscillates between 0 and 100. The Relative Strength of a stock's price action is the ratio of the moving averages of up periods divided by down periods. An up period is when the closing price of one period is <u>higher</u> than the closing price of the prior period. A down period is when the closing price of one period is <u>lower</u> than the closing price of the prior period. If a period is a down period, then the change in price is added to the down period moving average and a zero is added to the moving average of the up period.

Therefore:
> RS = Moving Average of Up periods / Moving Average of down periods

The index is then:
> RSI = 100 - [100/(1+RS)]

A stock that has had more AND larger positive price movement will have an RSI>50. A stock with only positive price movement every period will have zero down periods which means RS would be equal to infinity and the RSI would be 100 minus something close to zero and consequently approaching a value of 100.

The RSI was developed by J. Welles Wilder and first published in *New Concept in Technical Trading Systems* (1978). Yes, you too can create your own momentum indicator!

The RSI is most commonly used with a 14-day period otherwise called an RSI 14. The Oscillator has shown some accuracy of forecasting **overbought** conditions when the RSI>70 and **oversold** conditions when the RSI is <30.

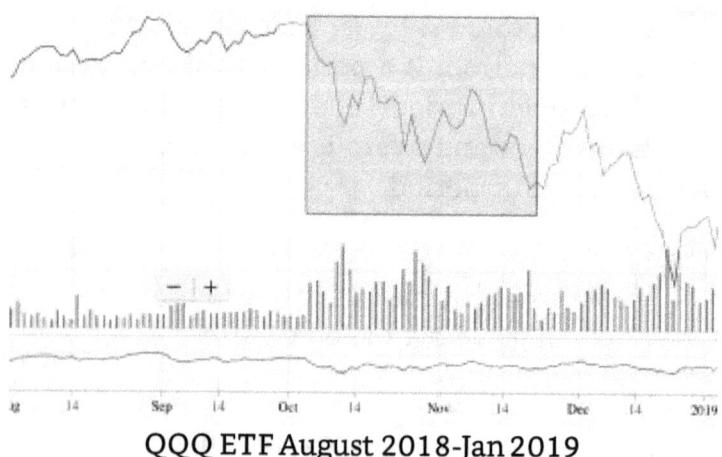

QQQ ETF August 2018-Jan 2019

When I first started using RSI to predict when to buy

a stock (RSI > 70) or sell it (RSI < 30) I started noticing two things:

1. It worked very well in smaller windows (5 min, 15 min, 30 min, and 1 hour)
2. The 70/30 was correct more times than not when the trend was SIDEWAYS

This second insight got me hypothecating what could really be happening in the market. The assumption is that when price changes very quickly (higher positive changes in a fixed period) then it must eventually mean that buying pressure will dry up and those same buyers will be looking to sell their shares because the price changes have decreased in magnitude. 70% buying strength relative to selling strength seems arbitrary but it's been shown to work in a sideways trend. Maybe it says something about our human behavior. After all, we tend to respond the same way to the same stimuli over and over in history. Well, I noticed that in bull runs, more people are buying and their optimism for where the price can go is higher meaning that they are less likely to start selling until a higher price point. This means that in a bull run or uptrend, overbought cannot be 70, and in fact it's much higher.

In an uptrend, I set my RSI to 80/50 and use 50 as a support level.

In a downtrend, I set my RSI to 50/20 and use 50 as my resistance level.

With experience, I came to find that adjusting the RSI based on whether the primary trend is an uptrend or a downtrend improves the RSI signal as a buy and sell signal. If we look at the QQQ chart when the stock moved from an uptrend to a downtrend in October 2018 we notice that the troughs of the RSI in the uptrend hovered around an RSI of 50, and during the downtrend the peaks hovered around an RSI 50 instead.

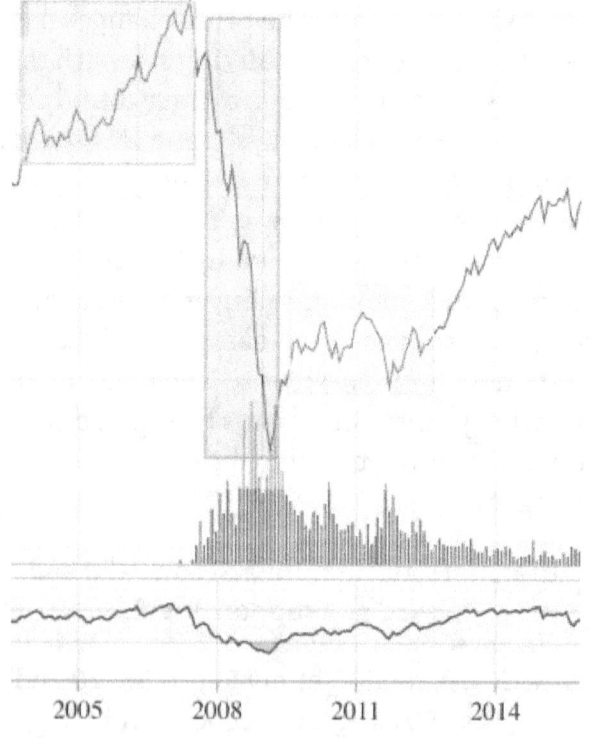

XLF 2005-2014

Similarly, in the XLF chart we see the same insights for a downtrend, uptrend, and sideways trends all highlighted on the chart. These types of insights are why I think it's important to build expertise in just a handful of indicators instead of learning all indicators but being an expert in none.

Additional insights from using the RSI indicator are the concepts of **divergence** and **reversals**. Divergence is when the price action and the RSI do not confirm each other. When price is in a downtrend and we find that the RSI is instead in an uptrend, that should be taken as a bullish signal. The opposite is true for a bearish signal when the price is in an uptrend making new highs but the RSI is in a downtrend making new lows. These are weak bullish and bearish signals that could signal temporary corrections rather than full reversals of trend. Reversal on the other have stronger signals. When a price is in a downtrend trend but the RSI oscillation has moved up above the RSI=50 line by showing higher lows then that is a bullish reversal signal. Similarly, when price is in an uptrend and the RSI oscillation drops below or around the RSI=50 line by showing lower lows then that is a bearish reversal signal.

CHART READING

If you have a brokerage account, you'll have access to any stock's advanced chart where you could automatically add technical indicators, trendlines, and even compare one price chart to another. Successful traders have habits that build lifelong knowledge. As such, there a few habits you need to adopt.

The first habit is you need to spend at least 30 minutes every day reading financial news. Online platforms to start with include:

- **https://www.economist.com/finance-and-economics/**
- **https://finance.yahoo.com/**

Additionally, there are several useful financial news apps including the CNBC Business News and Finance app, The MarketWatch app, and the Wall Street Journal.

The second habit is to begin a watchlist of stocks and ETFs you are interested in. The key is that you must be interested in them because you will find your knowledge compounding as you naturally read and learn more about the sector or the companies within the ETF that spark your interest. Download your broker's app and add a **universe** of stocks that you'll follow from now on. You can add and remove stocks as you gain confidence. Some of the most successful traders in the world only have a handful of stocks that they consistently trade.

The third habit you should adopt is to spend a few minutes every morning going over the price chart from the previous day or week of each of the stocks in your universe of stocks. Try and identify patterns, and see if you could have predicted price movements had you traded the stock. Stockchart-s.com and tradingview.com has an active community of amateur traders just as you who publish their technical analyses. You should search the ticker of one of the stocks in your universe to see if others could see the same pattern that you've identified. Be careful with these two sites because they can eat up a lot of your time, but do use them to compare notes with other traders.

With these three habits, you'll find that your under-standing and appreciation of price movement will significantly increase over time. Also be cognizant that you'll find only one or a handful of technical analyses that you come to prefer over time. That is a favorable outcome because even after learning the basics in this guide, you will find small nuances that are learned after months and years of read-ing charts. I've shared some insights I learned from using the RSI and MACD technical indicators in this guide to show you that you cannot be an expert in all types of technical analyses but you can be an expert in one or a handful.

When you first begin your journey in chart reading, you need to decide if you prefer viewing charts using an Arithmetic scale or a Logarithmic scale.

In an **Arithmetic Scale** the y-axis is made up of absolute numbers such that an increase in price from $10 to $20 and a price increase from $50 to $60 both move up the y-axis by 10 dollars. This is the traditional scale when stock charts are shown online.

In a **Logarithmic Scale** the y-axis is made up of percentage change. In this scale, a $10 change from $10 to $20 shows a 100% increase in the y-axis while the same absolute dollar change from $50 to $60 will show only a 20% increase in the y-axis.

Next you'll need to decide which **chart type** you prefer the most. There are four traditional chart types used to visualize buying and selling powers or the strength of the bulls and bears in the market. The chart types are line charts, bar charts, candlestick charts, and point and figure charts (reportedly originally developed by Charles Dow).

Next, you'll need to switch to **multiple windows**. For swing trading, use the 12 hour, 24 hour, and 1 week windows. Identify if the price action is in a downtrend or an uptrend. When each new peak is lower than the previous one, or as traders call it, 'lower highs' then the stock price is said to be in a downtrend. There is stronger conviction of calling the price movement a downtrend when the troughs are also lower or as traders call it 'lower lows'. The opposite is true of uptrends and these describe higher highs and higher lows.

Next, draw the **support** and **resistance** levels using either the trendlines, moving averages, or fixed price levels. You can do this mentally in a matter of seconds.

At this stage you would load your favorite technical indicators, and note four elements which are divergence, convergence, breakouts, and false breakouts. A **divergence** is when the price and a chosen technical indicator are moving in opposite directions. A **convergence** is when the price and a chosen technical indicator are moving in the same direction. A **bull breakout** is when price breaks above a resistance level usually followed with increased volume which increases the volatility of the stock and the percentage gain. A **bear breakout** is the opposite when price breaks below a support level and followed with increased volume. They are called breakouts because the next support or resistance is either far away enough or confirmed too long ago that there is no established support or resistance beyond the breakout. Note, a **false breakout** is when there isn't enough momentum (volume and price change) following the initial breakout which causes trades to close (sell) their position. False breakouts are common when trading gaps, and we will discuss gap trading in a later section.

With that we are ready to review some charts and figures. Use the next section as a reference as you complete your daily or weekly three habits. Learning today is only half the education, you have to see these concepts repeatedly in your chart readings until they become second nature and you can spot them within seconds of looking at the price action on a chart.

SECTION TWO

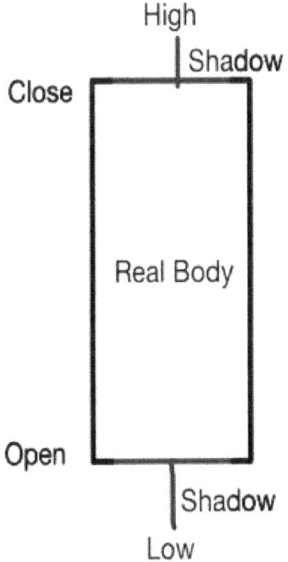

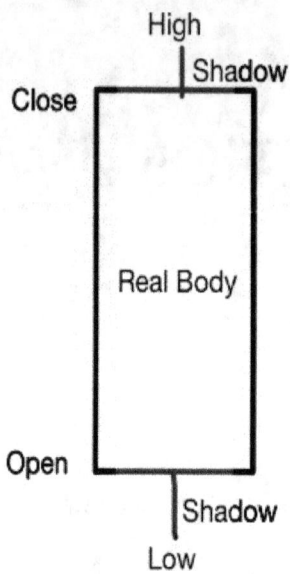

As a reminder, the candlestick gives us information on the price action for each period by displaying <u>all four price data points</u> in a single candlestick. The **real body** is **hollow** or clear if the closing price was higher than the opening price. The real body is **filled** if the closing price is lower than the opening price. This was a quick way to tell the price direction of each candlestick back in the black and white era. Today, modern candlestick charts fill the body with either green or red to indicate price movement relative to the <u>previous</u> close price. If the open is higher than the prior close then the candlestick is green, and if the open is lower than the prior close then the candlestick is red.

An important point to note is that trading days on the US exchanges begin at 9:30 am and end at 4 pm. That is 6.5 hours of trading activity. When choosing the periods for your candlesticks make sure they are a factor of 6.5 to get equally weighted candlesticks. In other words you can use 15, 30, or **65** minute periods but not 60 minute periods.

Let's next explore several popular candlestick patterns.

Hammer: The hammer is similar to a dragonfly but occurs after the price has dropped significantly below its previous lows but ends up at or near its opening price. It should be near enough the opening price so that the real body is ⅓ or less of the length of the lower shadow. A hammer needs confirmation of price action by seeing that the next period candlestick real body moved to a higher price point.

Shooting Star: This is similar to a gravestone doji following an uptrend where the closing price is below the opening price or close to it and the high price creates a long upper shadow that is at least twice as long as the real body. The difference is in the <u>size</u> of the real body, where it is almost non-existent in a gravestone doji but can be small in a shooting star as long as the upper shadow is at least twice the length of the body.

Hanging Man: This is a hammer candlestick pattern that occurs AFTER an uptrend and is a bearish signal. Notice the longer real body but also notice the long shadow showing serious indecision after an uptrend.

THE DOJIS

The Dojis are candlesticks with no bodies! The opening price is close to or identical to the closing price with either an upper shadow for a higher high price and/or a lower shadow for a lower low price in the same period. This spells INDECISION. When you see Dojis, think indecision between the buyers and sellers or the bulls and the bears. The price fluctuated significantly hence the long shadows but ultimately the closing price was the same as the opening price. Indecision is ominous for potential trend reversal or the bulls and bears are waiting on news such as FDA approval or denial for a biotech public company. The names that traders came up with to describe the different types of indecisions are very creative. Let's look at the main ones.

Dragonfly Doji: This is a candlestick pattern that shows a bullish trend. When the highs, the opening and the closing prices are very close with a long range (or shadow) then we get what looks like a dragonfly. This signals indecision between the bulls and bears on where the price should be and this indecision ultimately led to a higher price which indicates the bulls won.

Gravestone Doji: This is the opposite of a Dragonfly pattern in that the lows, opening, and closing prices are very close but the price range was wide again indicating indecision but ultimately ending <u>lower</u>. This is a bearish pattern that signals after indecision the bears won. It also looks like a gravestone.

CHART PATTERN RECOGNITION

There are many *many* different types of chart patterns that can be recognized when looking at the price action of a stock. I'll share a few of the most common ones. These patterns are divided into **continuation patterns** which means they signal continuation of the prior trend whether it is an uptrend or a downtrend and into **reversal patterns**. You will see reference to a bullish or bearish continuation pattern and a bullish or bearish reversal pattern depending on what the prior trend looked like.

CONTINUATION PATTERNS

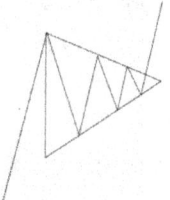

A **symmetrical** triangle depicts converging trend lines and signal continuation of the prior trend once the price breaks 'out' of the triangle.

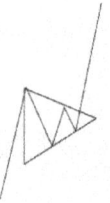

A **pennant** is made up of a symmetrical triangle that contains a small number, usually 1 to 3 cycles of price action. Note the prior trend (whether an uptrend or downtrend) is known as the pole.

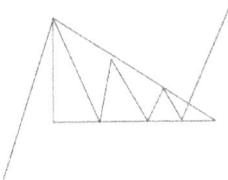

A **Descending triangle** has a horizontal lower trend which can be thought of as the support and a down-trending upper trend.

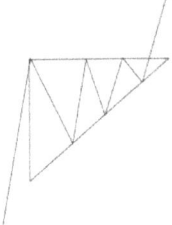

An **ascending triangle** has a horizontal upper trend which can be thought of as the resistance and an uptrending lower trend. An ascending triangle is a trader favorite because 'lower lows' are created by the price as it gets close to resistance meaning it is building up enough upwards momentum to break through the resistance.

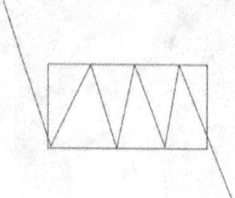

A **rectangle** is a sideways pattern which means indecision between the bulls and bears which likely means the prior trend will continue. Rectangles create resistance and support levels but once the support level is broken, it becomes a new resistance.

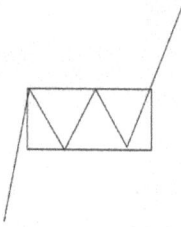

A **flag** is similar to the pennant in that it only contains a small number of cycles but instead of a symmetrical triangle, it forms a rectangle. The prior trend is also known as the pole. Remember, traders use the price change of the pole to come up with price targets when there is no support or resistance after the breakout.

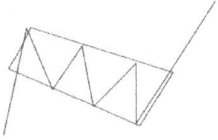

A **falling wedge** is when both trendlines are down-trending with expectation that the prior trend will continue. When the prior trend is an uptrend, this looks like a bullish flag.

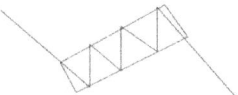

Similarly, a **rising wedge** is when both trendlines are uptrending with expectation that the trend will continue.

REVERSAL PATTERNS

QQQ July 2007-January 2008

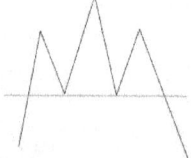

Head and Shoulders is a trend reversal pattern. In

a bearish reversal, we see three peaks, two for the shoulders and the middle peak for the head. The support level connecting all the lows of a head and shoulder pattern is called the neckline. Price must break below the neckline for a trend reversal of a prior uptrend. Note that a bullish reversal is an inverted head and shoulders pattern.

The head and shoulder bearish reversal pattern we saw in the first guide in the investment series. We had looked at charts of the major indices plotting annual returns by year and we see that we just moved over the second shoulder in this bull market run in mid 2018.

The **Microphone** is a broadening pattern that should probably be called a megaphone. It shows increasing volatility which is a sign that the buyers and sellers are unsure if the prior trend will continue and has been seen in the past to predict a trend reversal.

The **cup and handle** pattern is a classic chart pattern. If you see the cup by itself which is a long drawn out bottom of the price action, then that by itself has been seen to precede a longer term trend reversal. A bottom cup also called a rounding bottom is a bullish trend reversal. It is also inappropriately called a Kardashian bottom. The opposite, or a rounding top is a bearish trend reversal. Most cups come with handles which is a minor correction before continuing the up trend. In fact, you probably realized that the handle looks like a falling wedge which is a continuation pattern! :)

Lastly, when price action tests a price level twice and bounces back up, we call it a double bottom. When it tests a price level three times and still bounces back up, we call it a triple bottom. This is a bullish reversal. If the price actions tests a new high multiple times, let's say in a triple top then that is a bearish reversal indicating that the bulls are not winning this battle with the resistance level. To clarify, we had mentioned that a rectangle and descending/ascending triangles are continuation patterns but they look similar to a triple bottom or triple top. Well, that's true except for a tiny slight difference. Each subsequent testing of the support in a triple bottom has a lower low (remember our candlesticks) while each subsequent testing of the resistance in a triple top has a slightly higher high. I know that's not much to give the trader confidence. I have seen volume pick up with each bounce away from the support and resistance line, and that adds fuel for a potential reversal in trend. Personally, I always try and confirm a chart pattern with momentum in the RSI and the VWAP.

PRICE TARGETS

When a resistance level is broken, how do you know what the next resistance level is going to be if the price is reaching new highs it hasn't reached before? Setting up price targets may lower your overall gain but helps secure gains in the event that the momentum reverses thereby lowering your risk. But how do we think of setting up price targets? Well when the classic methods of using trendlines and moving averages to draw new support and resistance levels in the future don't work as well, traders have turned to volume. Volume by price helps establish new support levels based on the assumption that a lot of volume of shares were bought at a specific price. This can also be revealed using the VWAP described earlier.

Another method of coming up with price targets is to assume similar volatility from the prior primary trend. If a stock moved up 10% then moved sideways for a few periods and finally broke resistance, then you could hypothecate that it will continue another 10% before hitting a new resistance. This type of thinking has worked for many traders because it assumes that the buyers of a particular stock share common behaviors including selling after the stock has appreciated 10% for example. These same buyers from the prior rally will show up in the next rally so the assumption goes. When evaluating price targets after a significant chart pattern emerges, we can use that same logic. For example, in a head and shoulders pattern, we come up with an expected price target based on the distance between the head and the neckline. Others have used the percentage change in price between the head and neckline as a more accurate measure for volatility. When encountering flags or pennants, technical analysts use the distance of the pole--in absolute dollar change or as a percentage of price, and then add that to the resistance level that was broken to calculate a new price target.

While measuring the most recent trend helps establish new price targets, many other traders prefer to use an average metric of volatility to help set new resistance levels. They use what is known as Average True Range or ATR. The ATR was developed by J. Welles Wilder the same trader who came up with the RSI directional indicator. The ATR was initially developed to track commodities which were pretty volatile in the 1970s. Today, the ATR is used in the more volatile cryptocurrency markets. I've used ATR for stocks, and the Turtles (which we'll discuss later) also used ATR to exit trades. The ATR is a moving average, typically with 14 periods. The average for each period is the average of three absolute values:

1. Current period high price minus the current period low price
2. Current period high price minus the previous close price
3. Current period low price minus the previous close price

GAPS

Gaps are literal gap ups or downs in price seen with exuberant excitement from buyers or sellers. For example, an earnings surprise announced after the market closes could result in a much higher open price the following trading day. These are rare but when they do occur, traders have noticed a pattern emerge. Mainly the pattern of breakaway gaps followed by continuation gaps and finally ending with an exhaustion gap but they can also happen in isolation.

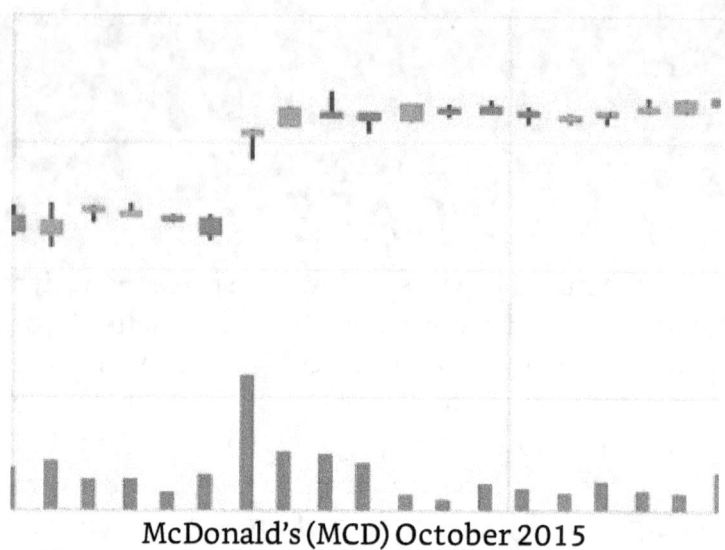

McDonald's (MCD) October 2015

A breakaway gap is a <u>reversal</u> of trend. For example, a stock could be trending sideways before a breakaway gap such as what occurred with McDonald's (MCD) in October 2015. The first candlestick after the gap up is a <u>hammer</u> as we learned earlier which is a bullish signal :) . These generally do not get filled. <u>Filling</u> a gap occurs when the initial irrational exuberance is realized to be irrational and a correction occurs where price returns to the previous period's close thereby filling the gap.

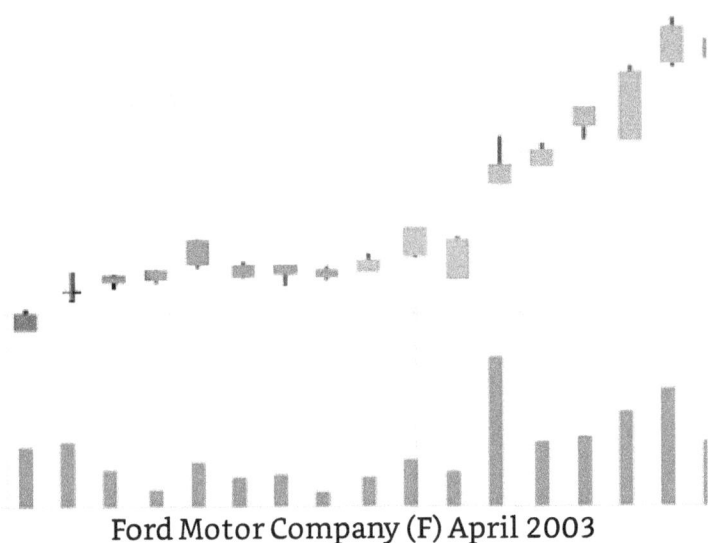

Ford Motor Company (F) April 2003

A continuation gap is also referred to as a runaway gap or a measuring gap. This gap is <u>continuation</u> of a trend. This is the second wave of buyers who missed out on the first opportunity to buy earlier in the trend. Notice the increase in volume during the gap up.

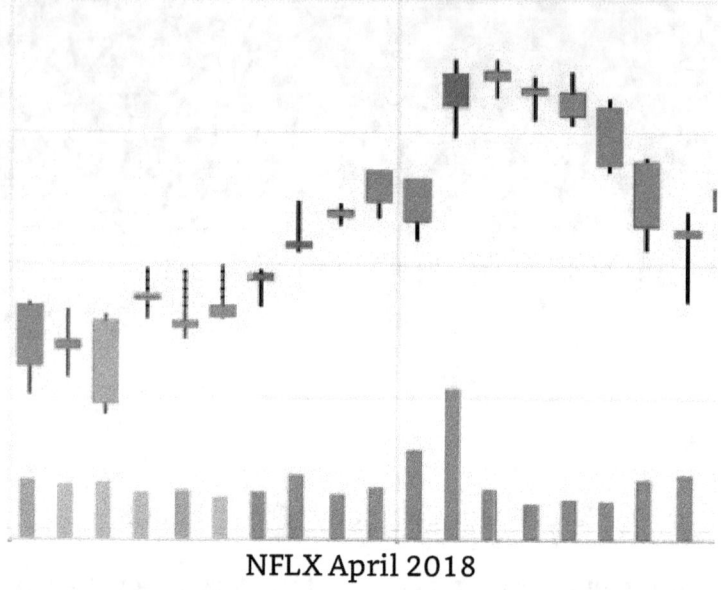

NFLX April 2018

An exhaustion gap occurs towards the <u>end</u> of a trend such as a rally. The third and final wave of buyers come in at this stage but the price either hits a new resistance level or the buyers from the first and second wave sell their shares causing downward pressure. As we can see in the Netflix price chart from April 2018, the exhaustion was filled very quickly soon after.

While in general gaps can be rarer, there are hundreds of stocks that keep showing gap after gap after gap. The Netflix price chart consistently shows exhaustion gaps and this may have to do with the behavior of the special type of buyer of the Netflix stock. The Waters (WAT) company which sells laboratory equipment consistently shows all three forms of gap ups and gap downs.

An important takeaway from trading gaps is to go back to the basics and understand the behavior of the market underlying this pattern. Remember, it is to your benefit to become an expert in a few technical indicators rather than a generalist in all indicators. The insights I've noticed trading gaps is that volume is slightly increased with continuation gaps and appears to be much higher for exhaustion gaps. Additionally, breakaway gaps are more likely when there is a prolonged period of accumulation during a sideways trend. I generally don't trade continuation and exhaustion gaps. I prefer breakaway gaps but even for those I make sure to pay attention where the resistance level is above the gap. If the gap up is still far away from the next resistance level, then I would trade it and my exit would be either at the next resistance level or twice of the ATR from the previous rally.

Trading gaps is a higher risk higher reward strategy and should be reserved for more experienced traders. You don't want to be a Netflix bag holder always buying in at the end of a trend.

FIBONACCI SEQUENCE

In 1202, the Italian mathematician Leonardo of Pisa later known as Fibonacci, published the Fibonacci sequence in his book Liber Abaci which translates to "The Book of Calculation". It is in the Liber Abaci that Fibonacci introduces the western world to the Indian digits of 1-9 and the Arabic 0 (zero) to facilitate calculations instead of using roman numerals which were impossible when it came to the study of calculations.

The Fibonacci sequence was just an observation in nature. What makes it special is that subsequent scholars found the sequence expressed much more often in nature such as the branching of trees, and the flowering of an artichoke. What is even more amazing is the sequence is one step away from expressing the **golden ratio** which is another repeated pattern in nature.

Fibonacci wanted to calculate the growth of a rabbit population. The whole explanation is hypothetical and does not even make sense biologically since a rabbit can have a littler as large as 14 rabbits with an average gestation of 1 month per litter. Still, Fibonacci assumed that each litter will produce 2 offspring, one male and one female, and that it takes one month to reach the age of maturity. In this hypothetical scenario, Fibonacci buys a pair of newly born rabbits in the first month, therefore has 1 pair of rabbits in month 1. In month 2, the rabbits mate but no offspring is produced yet until month 3 at which point we now have two pairs of rabbits (the parents and the offspring). In month three, the parents produce another pair of offspring (because the first set need another month to mature before they can mate). This leads to 3 pairs in the fourth month. And so on and so forth. In the first 12 months, the number of pairs of rabbits is as follows:

$$1,1,2,3,5,8,13,21,34,55,89,144$$

There is so much to say about how this pattern of numbers was then found in nature but I'll keep it brief. Remember my point earlier in the guide that if you try hard enough you will find patterns in anything? Well, that's exactly what mathematicians did.

First, if we divide any number in the sequence to the first number on its left such as 8/5 or 21/13 or 144/89 we get approximations to the **golden ratio** of **1.618**. The golden ratio in mathematics is one where a>b and a+b/a must equal a/b. In this case 8/5 must equal (8+5)/8 which is true since in the Fibonacci sequence whether 8 is divided by 5 or 13 is divided by 8, any division of one number in the sequence with the number to its left will yield the golden ratio!

What if we reverse the order and divide a number to the number on its right such as 5/8, 13/21, or 89/144? Well we get **0.618**. Okay, what if we divide a number to a number two spaces to its left in the sequence such as 5/2, 13/5, or 144/55? We get **2.618**. If we do the same thing with three numbers to the left we get 4.236. Again (final one I promise) if we divide a number with four numbers to the left in the sequence, we get **6.854**.

Now interestingly, we find that the golden ratio of 1.618 squared is 2.618. Similarly, 1.618^3 is 4.236 and 1.618^4 is 6.854! Fun with numbers.

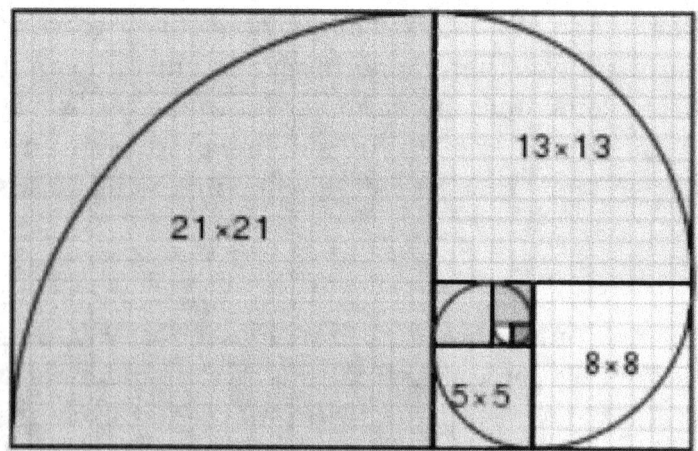

Mathematicians then decided to draw the Fibonacci sequence in squares with a side equal to a number in the sequence. They would draw a 1x1 square, then another 1x1 square, then a 2x2 square, and so on. It turns out that adding two Fibonacci numbers together in a sequence gives us the subsequent number in the sequence, represented here by adding two sides of two consecutive squares (5 and 8) is equivalent to the side of the 13x13 square. More interestingly, is the quarter circle that connects the two corners of each square. If we draw a quarter circle in each square we end up with a spiral whose length per each quarter turn is exactly the golden ratio (1.618) multiplied by the side of the square. This same pattern is seen in sea shells where each turn produces a larger radius that is a <u>factor</u> of the golden ratio.

The Fibonacci sequence has also been attributed to flowers having specific petals such that lilies and iris have 3 petals, buttercups have 5 petals, some delphiniums have 8 and corn marigolds have 13 petals.

While the topic requires a much lengthier discussion, let's return to how traders have found the Fibonacci pattern in the price action of a stock.

If we notice a trend reversal, then a **Fibonacci retracement** can occur to a price down to 61.8% from the peak.

If we notice a trend continuation, then a **Fibonacci**

extension reveals price targets at 161.8% from the beginning of the trend, as well as subsequent price targets of 261.8%, 423.6%, and 685.4%. These price targets act as resistance levels. If a price action breaks through the first Fibonacci extension of 161.8%, then expect it to move to the next resistance level of 261.8% from the beginning of the initial trend. Personally, I've found that if I already have support and resistance levels drawn, then if a support or resistance level happens <u>to also be</u> a Fibonacci retracement or extension, that boosts my confidence. Otherwise, when there is no support or resistance level I can rely on, using the Fibonacci sequence as a scaffold to visualize my exit strategy is helpful.

RE-ENTRY & THE TURTLE TRADERS

"Richard J. Dennis
Of C&D Commodities
is accepting applications for the position of
Commodity Futures Trader
to expand his established group of traders."

Wall Street Journal, 1984

By now most traders have heard of the phenomenal story of the turtle traders. If you haven't, here's a short summary. Richard Dennis and William Eckhardt, highly successful commodity traders had a debate on whether successful trading requires natural talent or if instead it is something that can be taught to anyone. Dennis himself had turned $5000 into $200 million trading commodity futures on the Chicago trading floors by the age of 37 years old. It took him only 15 years of trading. Dennis believed that anyone could be taught a set of fixed rules and through those rules trade successfully. In 1983, Dennis and Eckhardt decided to settle the debate by recruiting 14 students from all walks of life (diversity was key for this experiment) who underwent a two week training trading course using Dennis' own cash. The students were called turtles because Dennis had visited a turtle breeding farm in Singapore, and thought 'turtles' was a great nickname because like in Singapore, he would be growing turtles.

There were only two classes of turtles--in 1983 and 1984. There were liberals, conservatives, MBA graduates, highschool graduates, bartenders, board game designers, phone clerks, and even one student who simply stated his occupation as 'unemployed'. The experiment ended after that, and the majority of students who continued to trade using Dennis's system became multimillionaires. For example, R. Jerry Parker, an accountant, learned under Dennis in 1985 when he was 25 years old. 10 years later, he earned $35 million from trading in one year. The book *The Complete TurtleTrader* by Michael Covel goes into detail on some of the most successful turtles and where they are now. In the first 5 years after learning to trade, the turtles earned $175 million. The turtle trading system was a secret and the turtle traders have modified and improved upon the system over the years branching beyond commodities and into other asset classes.

There are a few things we do know. Dennis taught the turtles to go long on breakouts and short breakdowns. He taught them to only risk a small portion of their account per trade-generally 2%. Instead of chart patterns (such as the head and shoulders and other reversal patterns we learned about), Dennis taught the turtles to use a proxy for the moving average. They would buy at the new 20 period high price and sell at the new 10 period low price. That means they had to record the open, high, low, and close price each day. Lastly, an important lesson he taught the turtles was to plan their <u>exit strategy</u> while they are planning their entry into a stock.

Setting price targets and using fixed price resistance levels is one way of deciding when to exit before you enter a trade. So is using Fibonacci prior to entering a trade. Recognizing candlesticks and chart patterns are methods of deciding when to exit <u>while</u> in a trade. Another method is to consider each stock's inherent volatility. Dennis taught his students to exit the trade if it moves against them by 2 times the average volatility--or in other words, to place a stop loss order today that is twice the ATR (Average True Range) for every trade. To protect their winnings as they waited for the new 10 period low, they would move their exit point up as the stock moved up. Today, we would move the stop loss up so it remained 2 ATR below the new price IF the stock moved up a full ATR. These ratios are given as examples, traders choose any number of volatility measures, and the ones who use the ATR likely have changed the ATR ratio for different stocks.

RISK MANAGEMENT

Risk management is a very important tool when trading stocks. There are countless books and on-line courses solely focused on risk management. I will simplify it. First, it is fundamental to understand that technical trading is based on the belief or assumption that our trades succeed more than 50% of the time. That means many of our trades will fail. A lot of them will fail. Risk management is concerned with minimizing those losses. Having said, if our trading strategy works more than 50% of the time (get this one right first), THEN a simple risk management strategy is to follow these three tenants:

1. Bet the same dollar value per stock. Alternatively, you could decide to bet 5% of your total portfolio on each trade. Stay consistent with the same fixed absolute value or percentage bet.
2. Sell if the <u>trend changes</u> OR place a stop loss at ½ to 2 times the volatility.
3. If the trend is moving where you ex-

pected it to go, move your stop loss up.

Review your wins and losses frequently. Always keep your statistic, your metric, your ratio of wins vs. losses always up to date. Are you a 51% trader? Are you a 57.5% trader? Are you profitable at these levels? Maybe you're only profitable if you win 60% of the time? You may need to adjust your stop loss for the losers, and where you exit for the winners. The point is that you have to know how successful of a trader you are because if you can stay consistent, then you can potentially make a living solely from trading.

CONCLUSION

We learned a lot but we also barely scratched the surface. I shared some of the common technical analyses and some of my favorite ones. What I hope you take from this guide is to think of price action as telling a story of human behavior. Additionally, any pattern that works or you've noticed working must be working because of some underlying human behavior. As you begin to test different candlestick patterns, chart patterns, and any of a more than a hundred different technical indicators, pick one or just a handful and focus on these for several weeks until you gain some additional insights about the behavior of the market. Some of the best traders only use a few indicators. A messy chart means you are throwing everything at the chart and hoping something sticks in retrospect. Be disciplined. Be diligent. It takes a little bit of practice reviewing charts before it finally clicks and you see all sorts of patterns in a matter of seconds. That's when you begin to almost visualize all sorts of human interactions, thoughts, emotions, and reasoning that took place before the orders were placed.

There are a few traders who consistently beat the

index and have returns of 20-25% every year. Some as high as 100% every year (a few of the turtle traders for example). As long as you protect yourself from losses and gradually improve your trader score, you could semi-retire and continue trading out of passion. It is unfortunately an almost zero sum game, so someone must lose for another person to win (excluding the fees the exchanges and brokers make for every trade). On the other hand, if the economy continues to go up then trading is like passing along virtual paper from one person to another person who pays more for it until the last person has no one to sell it to or the company itself goes bankrupt. Acknowledging that it is a zero sum game is important to understand that the ones who are always making money in this game are the people selling access and the companies crowd-funding millions during their IPO. Then there are people who make money more often than not but never always. That is us. We need to find a pattern that works for the types of stocks we naturally are inclined to trade and make a profit so we could make money work for us.

Hopefully you enjoyed reading this guide on trading as I enjoyed writing about and sharing my knowledge. I should say that while everything taught in this guide can be used for day trading, I have primarily used the analyses for swing trading using the 1-day and 1-week time intervals. This allows me to trade only a few times a month, and affords me time

Peter Oliver

to enjoy working on other pursuits.

Trading is a lifelong journey. Once you start, it'll be hard to stop especially if you created a new source of income and have newfound prosperity. Please take a few minutes to join the free community at https://www.concisereads.com/ to discuss trading and share ideas among other CR readers. Unlike other trading books, there is no 'advanced' course that will cost you hundreds of dollars. It's free to join and free to participate. Well it costs me a pretty penny to maintain the servers, but a small price to pay to get folks openly engaging in dialogue. Hope to see you there!

--- The End ---

ADDITIONAL MATERIAL

Summary chart and candlestick patterns have been uploaded to https://www.concisereads.com . Any additional charts I create will be uploaded there as well.